Nicolas Barber

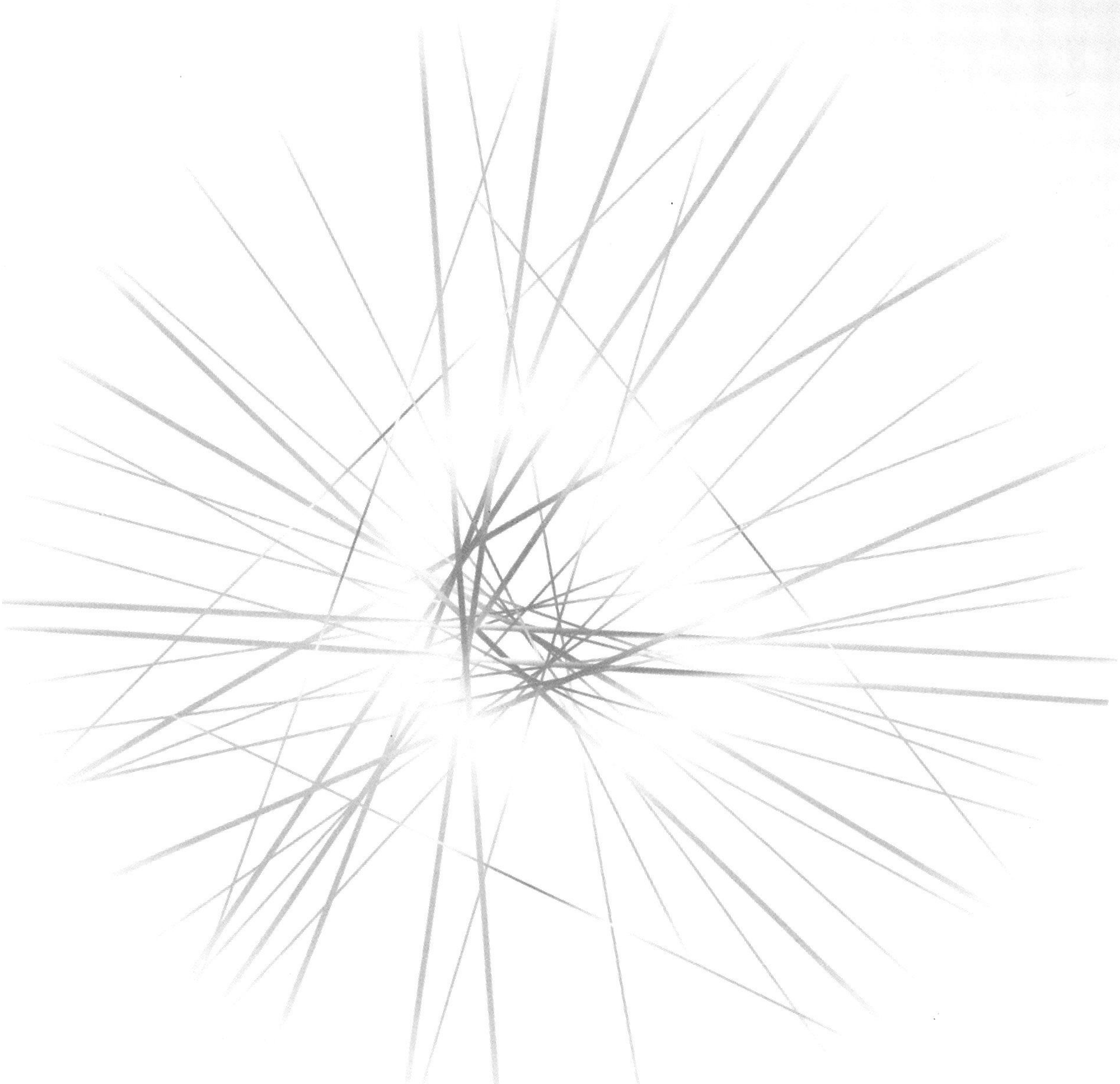

# ESSENTIALS

## Year 7
## KS3 English
### Workbook

# How to Use this Workbook

## A Note to the Teacher

This is the first of three English workbooks for students in Key Stage 3. Together, the workbooks for Years 7, 8 and 9 provide practice of the complete programme of study for Key Stage 3 English.

Included in the centre of the book is a pull-out answer booklet. It contains the answers to all of the questions in this workbook.

The topics covered in this workbook complement the KS3 Year 7 English Essentials Coursebook to provide further practice and help consolidate learning. The coursebooks provide clear, concise information as well as further practice questions.

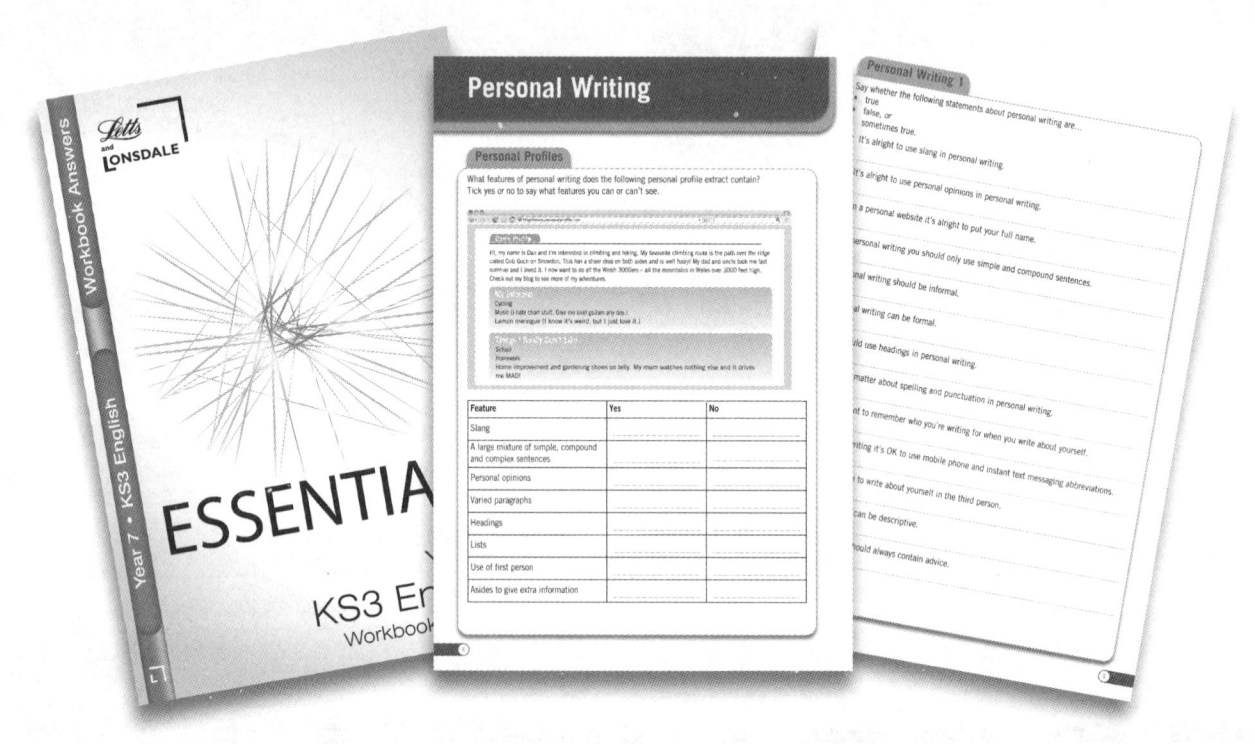

## A Note to the Student

We're sure you'll enjoy using this workbook, but follow these helpful hints to make the most of it:

- Try to write your answers in Standard English, using correct punctuation and good sentence construction. Read what you have written to make sure it makes sense.

- Some questions will require extra research, using reference books like dictionaries, encyclopedias and thesauruses, or the use of the internet.

- The tick boxes on the Contents page let you track your progress: simply put a tick in the box next to each topic when you've completed the exercises and questions.

# Contents

## Contents

# Personal Writing

## Personal Profiles

What features of personal writing does the following personal profile extract contain? Tick yes or no to say what features you can or can't see.

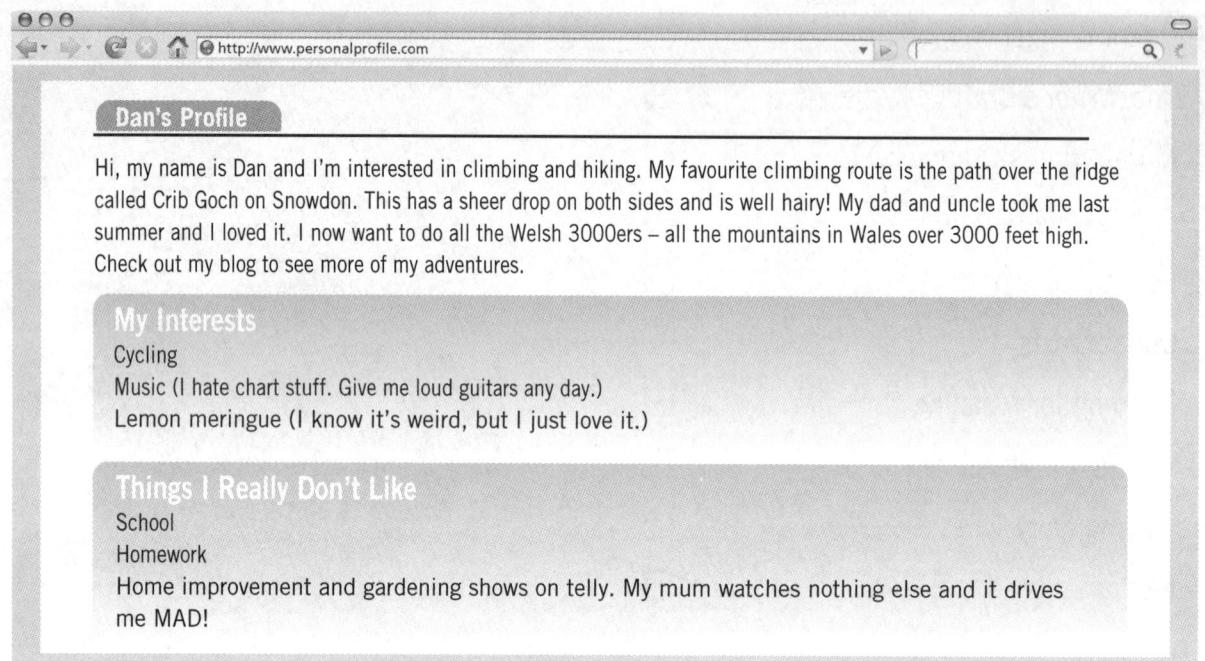

| Feature | Yes | No |
|---|---|---|
| Slang | | |
| A large mixture of simple, compound and complex sentences | | |
| Personal opinions | | |
| Varied paragraphs | | |
| Headings | | |
| Lists | | |
| Use of first person | | |
| Asides to give extra information | | |

## Personal Writing 1

Say whether the following statements about personal writing are...

- true
- false, *or*
- sometimes true.

**a)** It's alright to use slang in personal writing.

**b)** It's alright to use personal opinions in personal writing.

**c)** On a personal website it's alright to put your full name.

**d)** In personal writing you should only use simple and compound sentences.

**e)** Personal writing should be informal.

**f)** Personal writing can be formal.

**g)** You should use headings in personal writing.

**h)** It doesn't matter about spelling and punctuation in personal writing.

**i)** It's important to remember who you're writing for when you write about yourself.

**j)** In personal writing it's OK to use mobile phone and instant text messaging abbreviations.

**k)** It isn't possible to write about yourself in the third person.

**l)** Personal writing can be descriptive.

**m)** Personal writing should always contain advice.

**1** Circle the correct options in the following sentences:

**a)** A personal profile is something that's becoming more and more popular due to the increase in **chat / messaging / social networking** sites on the internet. These sites allow people to **promote / discover / rearrange** themselves to anyone who's interested.

**b)** Personal profiles aren't new and have been used in magazines and newspapers for a long time. One well-known type is the kind still found in football match-day **diaries / programmes / lists** and in teenage **newspapers / phones / magazines**, where a celebrity answers questions in order to give the reader a sense of their likes and dislikes.

**c)** There are many other types of personal writing. On the internet, a **board / forum / blog** – short for 'weblog'– is a type of **board / diary / newspaper**, but one that can be read by lots of people and not just the person who wrote it.

**d)** People have lost their jobs for posting comments about their bosses online when it was read by someone they didn't want to read it! This shows how important it is to keep in mind the **boss / law / audience** that you're writing for and the effect that you have upon them.

**e)** A **journal / newspaper / lawsuit** is a kind of diary that can be written down or posted online. It tends to be a bit more **informal / formal / annoying** than a diary and may be designed for others to read. Nowadays, many people see little difference between them and you may see the two names used for both types of writing.

**f)** A(n) **autobiography / biography / anecdote** is a much longer piece of personal writing which is about your entire life so far, written by yourself. Not everyone can be relied on to tell the truth – many writers **exaggerate / tell the truth / generalise** in order to make their lives sound more interesting or to make themselves sound better than they really are!

**2** Look at this example of personal writing and, using different colours, underline examples of the following:

**Slang**     **Personal opinion**     **Emotive language**     **Anecdote**     **Exaggeration**

---

# 18th April

I couldn't be bothered with anything today. Everyone got on my wick. I desperately wanted to go out, but no-one else was interested. It's happened millions and millions of times before – I want to do something, but nobody else does. It's like the time that I wanted to go to the zoo – several of my mates had said they fancied going, but when it came down to it, did they bother? No. Today was like that.

---

| D | D | W | M | A | M | Y | F | O | R | O | I | G |
|---|---|---|---|---|---|---|---|---|---|---|---|---|
| I | V | S | T | O | R | Y | M | N | L | U | K | I |
| A | E | C | F | K | L | S | R | I | O | M | E | M |
| R | U | E | E | P | D | E | O | N | G | D | S | K |
| Y | T | S | J | R | J | N | J | B | B | M | Y | I |
| E | D | I | T | O | R | I | A | L | O | E | O | T |
| F | I | U | G | F | U | U | P | O | O | D | N | L |
| A | B | Q | K | I | X | R | O | G | K | N | R | P |
| L | N | R | H | L | B | E | N | A | E | F | E | O |
| S | B | K | S | E | Y | I | Z | A | P | I | K | E |
| S | T | A | T | E | M | E | N | T | L | E | M | T |
| R | C | O | M | A | B | R | N | S | E | Y | S | R |
| A | U | T | O | B | I | O | G | R | A | P | H | Y |

Use the following clues to find 11 different types of personal writing in the word search. The first one has been done for you.

**a)** You might write one day-by-day.       *diary*

**b)** Written by the person in charge of a newspaper.

**c)** Written by someone to sum up and show off their character, perhaps on the internet.

**d)** A formal diary.

**e)** An internet diary.

**f)** A written text that you might give to the police.

**g)** A book written about you, by you.

**h)** Verse.

**i)** A prose account telling a tale.

**j)** A personal account of a life, often written later in life.

**k)** A set of observations about events.

# Shakespeare

## Shakespeare's Life

The following passage contains 10 factual errors about Shakespeare's life.
Find the errors and write them in the spaces below.

William Shakespeare was born in Stoke-on-Trent in Warwickshire in 1564. His mother was the daughter of a well-off landowner and his father was involved in the glove-making trade. Shakespeare probably went to the comprehensive school in Stratford-upon-Avon.

The next event in his life we can be certain of was his divorce in 1582 to a farmer's daughter, Anne Hathaway. They had a baby girl in 1583 and triplets in 1585, two years after their first child. After this time, there are virtually no records of what happened in his life – these are often called his 'lost' years. The next recorded mention of him is in 1592, when he is documented as being a theatre worker.

As an actor, Shakespeare was connected to the Lord Playwright's Company. This changed its name in 1603 to the King's Company when King Albert came to the throne. The Company was financially involved in two theatres in Tottenham, both of which were near to the river Thames. These theatres were called the Globe and the Blackfriars.

Although Shakespeare is mainly famous for his plays, it was his poetry that was published first, in 1593 and 1594. A large number of Shakespeare's novels were presumably written around this time too – the first written evidence of plays by Shakespeare occurs in 1594 and from then until 1611 he seemed to write about two plays a year. Among the first plays he wrote are *Titus Andronicus* and *A Midsummer Night's Dream*. In the early 1600s he started to write more comedies such as *Hamlet*, *King Lear* and *Othello*. From 1608 onwards, his later plays such as *Cymbeline* and *The Tempest* seem to have been written.

At the end of his life he returned to Stratford having made his fortune. He died on his birthday, 23rd April, in 1616. On his tomb in Holy Trinity Church, Burslem, there is a rhyme threatening to curse anyone who disturbs his bones! Seven years after his death in 1623 the first collected edition of his works was published.

a) ...........................................................................................................

b) ...........................................................................................................

c) ...........................................................................................................

d) ...........................................................................................................

e) ...........................................................................................................

f) ...........................................................................................................

g) ...........................................................................................................

h) ...........................................................................................................

i) ...........................................................................................................

j) ...........................................................................................................

## Shakespeare's Theatre

Read the description of the Globe Theatre and answer the questions that follow.

The Globe was built in 1599 using wood from an earlier theatre, that had been built by Richard Burbage's father, James Burbage, in Shoreditch in 1576. Originally the Burbages had a 21-year lease of the site on which The Theatre was built. After problems with the lease-holder when it expired, they dismantled The Theatre piece by piece and transported it over the Thames, where they reconstructed it as the Globe.

On June 29, 1613, the Globe Theatre was set alight during a play. A theatrical cannon, set off during a performance of Henry the Eighth, misfired, which ignited the wooden beams and the roof-thatch. According to one of the few surviving documents, the only casualty was a man who extinguished his burning trousers with a bottle of beer!

The Globe was rebuilt in 1614, but was closed down by the Puritans in 1642, like they had done to all the other London theatres. In 1644 the Globe was destroyed to make room for poor quality housing called tenements. The precise location of the Globe was unknown until 1989, when some of its foundations were discovered beneath the car park of Anchor Terrace on Park Street (the shape of the foundations are replicated in the car park's surface). There could be further remains beneath Anchor Terrace, but the 18th-century terrace is listed so archaeologists aren't allowed to dig there.

The actual dimensions of the Globe are unknown, but its shape and size can be estimated from research and the theories of those who have studied it over the past two centuries. Evidence suggests that it was a three-storey, open-air amphitheatre between 97 and 102 feet (29.6–31.1m) in diameter that could hold up to 3,000 spectators. Wenceslas Hollar's sketch of the Globe shows the building as being a circular shape (He later incorporated his sketch into his engraved 'Long View' picture of London in 1647). However, many years later, in 1997-98, a small part of the Globe's foundations was uncovered that suggested the Globe was a polygon of 18 or 20 sides.

a) Why wasn't the Globe Theatre an original building?

b) Why didn't the rebuilt Globe last very long?

c) According to this extract, why do we know so little about the Globe?

d) Why aren't archaeologists allowed to dig up the Globe?

e) Why might there be disagreement over the shape of the Globe?

f) Who was the Globe closed down by?

g) Which family were involved in the building of the Globe?

## Modern Meanings

Read this extract from *Romeo and Juliet* and match the words in bold with their meanings in the table below.

PROLOGUE

Two **households**, both alike in dignity,
In fair Verona, where we lay our scene,
From **ancient grudge** break to **new mutiny**,
Where **civil blood** makes civil hands unclean.
From forth the **fatal loins** of these two foes
A pair of **star-cross'd** lovers take their life;
Whole **misadventured** piteous overthrows
Do with their death bury their parents' **strife**.
The fearful passage of their death-mark'd love,
And the **continuance** of their parents' rage,
Which, but their children's end, **nought** could remove,
Is now the two hours' **traffic** of our stage;
The which if you with patient ears **attend**,
What here shall miss, our **toil** shall strive to mend.

| Meaning | Word |
|---|---|
| Ill-fated | a) |
| Families | b) |
| Ordinary people's suffering | c) |
| Hard work | d) |
| Badly affected | e) |
| Listen carefully | f) |
| Old quarrel | g) |
| Carrying on | h) |
| Fresh disturbances | i) |
| Jinxed families | j) |
| Nothing | k) |
| Trouble | l) |
| Action | m) |

## Shakespeare's Vocabulary

Here are a number of phrases associated with Shakespeare. What do you think each one means?

**a)** All that glitters is not gold.

**b)** As merry as the day is long.

**c)** As pure as the driven snow.

**d)** At one fel! swoop.

**e)** Frailty thy name is woman.

**f)** Foul play.

**g)** I have not slept one wink.

**h)** I bear a charmed life.

**i)** I want my pound of flesh.

**j)** Snatched out of the jaws of death.

# Genre & Science Fiction

## Science Fiction

Read the following extract from *The Time Machine* by H.G. Wells and give five reasons why it is a science fiction text.

'Scientific people,' proceeded the Time Traveller, after the pause required for the proper assimilation of this, 'know very well that Time is only a kind of Space. Here is a popular scientific diagram, a weather record. This line I trace with my finger shows the movement of the barometer. Yesterday it was so high, yesterday night it fell, then this morning it rose again, and so gently upward to here. Surely the mercury did not trace this line in any of the dimensions of Space generally recognized? But certainly it traced such a line, and that line, therefore, we must conclude was along the Time-Dimension.'

'But,' said the Medical Man, staring hard at a coal in the fire, 'if Time is really only a fourth dimension of Space, why is it, and why has it always been, regarded as something different? And why cannot we move in Time as we move about in the other dimensions of Space?'

The Time Traveller smiled. 'Are you sure we can move freely in Space? Right and left we can go, backward and forward freely enough, and men always have done so. I admit we move freely in two dimensions. But how about up and down? Gravitation limits us there.'

'Not exactly,' said the Medical Man. 'There are balloons.'

'But before the balloons, save for spasmodic jumping and the inequalities of the surface, man had no freedom of vertical movement.'

'Still they could move a little up and down,' said the Medical Man.

'Easier, far easier down than up.'

'And you cannot move at all in Time, you cannot get away from the present moment.'

'My dear sir, that is just where you are wrong. That is just where the whole world has gone wrong. We are always getting away from the present movement. Our mental existences, which are immaterial and have no dimensions, are passing along the Time-Dimension with a uniform velocity from the cradle to the grave. Just as we should travel down if we began our existence fifty miles above the earth's surface.'

a) Reason 1

_____

b) Reason 2

_____

c) Reason 3

_____

d) Reason 4

_____

e) Reason 5

## Written Genres

Choose the correct genre from the options given to complete the following table.

Science fiction   Romance   Horror   Humour   Cowboy

Action adventure   Crime   Biography   Fantasy   History

| Genre | Features |
|---|---|
| a) | Dark vocabulary<br>Use of ellipsis<br>Short sentences to shock |
| b) | Long, descriptive sentences to create a mood of wide-open spaces<br>Short sentences to create tension<br>Gunfights |
| c) | Lots of verbs to create movement and thrills<br>Jungles<br>Journeys and chases |
| d) | Spaceships and aliens<br>The question, 'What if?'<br>Technological vocabulary |
| e) | Detectives<br>Ellipsis<br>Cliffhangers<br>Dark vocabulary |
| f) | Old-fashioned vocabulary<br>Castles and knights in armour |
| g) | Factual<br>Opinions<br>Descriptive<br>Chronological |
| h) | Language of love<br>Aimed more at female readers<br>Sentimental vocabulary |
| i) | Swords and sorcery<br>Strange made-up names<br>Lengthy descriptive sentences to create a feeling of another world |
| j) | Ridiculous contrasts<br>Exaggeration<br>People made to do unusual or funny things |

## Identifying Genres

What genre do you think the following passages belong to?
Give three reasons why you think they belong to that genre.

**a)**

> The looming red cliffs of the Grand Canyon stretched out in front of him. The canyon was like a gaping mouth, ready to swallow him up. It looked as big as a moon crater. Down below he could hear the wind whistling and he could see dust blowing at the edge of the trail. Carefully, he took the first steps down the cracked, crumbling path. His horse took nervous steps and the flies buzzed around his Stetson as they ventured downwards. From the distance came a sound like an animal, yet not an animal; a signal...

**i)** I think this is an example of the _____ genre.

**ii)** Reason 1

_____

Reason 2

_____

Reason 3

_____

**b)**

> The inky darkness of infinite space stretched far beyond him. All that held him safely to the craft was the oxygen supply and its accompanying rope. What if this was to break? Behind him shone the bright blue glow of Earth, silently pulling him back with its weakening gravitational force. Before him, after completing the repairs, was the greatest adventure of his life. Unbeknown to him, away to his left, a blinking green light was twitching and watching; waiting.

**i)** I think this is an example of the _____ genre.

**ii)** Reason 1

_____

Reason 2

_____

Reason 3

_____

## Identifying Genre from Vocabulary

Below are sets of vocabulary that you might use in, or associate with, a particular genre. Write the name of the genre that you think each list of vocabulary belongs to.

| Vocabulary | Genre to which it belongs |
|---|---|
| Murder<br>Criminal<br>Suspicious<br>Alleyway<br>Rain-soaked | a) |
| Once upon a time<br>Princess<br>Beautiful<br>Handsome<br>Evil | b) |
| Darling<br>Roses<br>Smooch<br>Delicate<br>Smitten | c) |
| Armour<br>Chariot<br>Clanking<br>Stone<br>Conquering | d) |
| Dragon<br>Sword<br>Quest<br>Creature<br>Ethereal | e) |
| Moon<br>Planet<br>Turbo-thruster<br>Alien<br>Sinister | f) |
| Outlaw<br>Tumbleweed<br>Horse<br>Cactus<br>Posse | g) |

# The Writer's Craft

## Similes

Draw lines between the boxes to match the common simile with its ending.

| Simile | Ending |
|--------|--------|
| **a)** As sly as a… | Lighting |
| **b)** As quiet as a… | Two peas in a pod |
| **c)** As heavy as… | Fiddle |
| **d)** As thin as a… | Fox |
| **e)** As deaf as a… | Mustard |
| **f)** As poor as a… | Kitten |
| **g)** As brave as a… | Houses |
| **h)** As fast as… | Lead |
| **i)** As playful as a… | Bird |
| **j)** As hungry as a… | Church mouse |
| **k)** As alike as… | Hatter |
| **l)** As fit as a… | Rock |
| **m)** As free as a… | Mouse |
| **n)** As innocent as a… | Fruitcake |
| **o)** As keen as… | Lion |
| **p)** As mad as a… | Rake |
| **q)** As nutty as a… | Old boots |
| **r)** As safe as… | Lamb |
| **s)** As solid as a… | Hippo |
| **t)** As tough as… | Post |

## Adjectives, Metaphors & Similes

**1** Read the following sentences and write down the adjectives.

   **a)** 'Dirty Old Dog' is the fabulous new single from Elvis Fontenot and the Sugar Bees.

   **b)** Godfrey's amazing disguise skills meant that he wasn't discovered.

   **c)** Little Tara's exciting job brought her immense satisfaction.

   **d)** The French police refused to let unlucky Rebecca into the country because she had lost her new passport.

   **e)** Old Mike's immaculate paintings were sold for vast amounts on the internet.

**2** Read the following sentences and say whether they contain a metaphor or a simile.

   **a)** Alan's fingers whizzed up and down the frets of the guitar like lightning.

   **b)** A cloud of gloom hung over the relegated team's fans.

   **c)** The relegated team's fans felt as depressed as a deflated balloon.

   **d)** The result was a sweet treat for fans of the winning team.

   **e)** Arthur was so glum he looked like he had swallowed his false teeth.

**3** Circle the most appropriate adjective in each of the following sentences to make the simile effective.

   **a)** Frances was as **happy / forgetful / jubilant** as a goldfish because she didn't buy a lottery ticket the week her numbers came up.

   **b)** Michelle was as excited as a **run-down / hyperactive / lazy** child when she got her first job.

## Descriptive Techniques 1

Read the following passage and find examples of the descriptive techniques below.

> Splash! Natasha accidentally dropped her shiny keys into the bucket of water, where they sank like a stone. The crashing, clinking sound of metal on tin echoed throughout the room. The dull thud of her footsteps was a depressed drumbeat of gloom that followed her to the kitchen, where she looked for her rubber gloves to fish out her keys.
>
> Outside, the sky cried in sympathy. Inside, the kitchen stool rocked back on its heels and crashed to the floor as Natasha knocked it over. It was a bad, sad, depressing day and it was getting worse.

**a)** Adjectives

**b)** Alliteration

**c)** Onomatopoeia

**d)** Assonance

**e)** Personification

**f)** Pathetic fallacy

**g)** Similes

**h)** Metaphors

## Descriptive Techniques 2

Read the following sentences and say what descriptive technique(s) is / are being used.

**a)** Horrible Horatio's happy holiday helped his mood.

**b)** Bang! Pow! The superhero whizzed through the doorway.

**c)** The flowers wilted, suffering from the intense heat.

**d)** The sky cried tears of joy as the sun peeped from behind the clouds.

**e)** The rowdy, gruff men stormed into the pub and ordered some stiff drinks.

**f)** The girls were as happy as two-time lottery winners with the dresses they'd bought in the sales.

**g)** The cloud had a silver lining when it was revealed they were due a big insurance payout.

**h)** Crack! The twig snapped with a sound like a popped crisp packet.

**i)** The dull thud rumbled across the room.

**j)** The resounding rumble of racing rocks was heard throughout the mountains.

**k)** A cloud of gloom hung over the losing team's supporters.

**l)** The gentle, calm atmosphere soothed their nerves.

**m)** The dark, threatening, ominous clouds filled the sky.

**n)** Raging Rodney's remarks rattled the reporter.

# More Writer's Craft

## Verbs

Here are a number of sentences with a choice of verbs.
Choose the most descriptive and interesting verb.

a)  Catherine **walked** / **strolled** to the shop.

b)  Liam **hammered** / **knocked** on the door.

c)  Joe **sat** / **collapsed** at his desk.

d)  Alexandra **ate** / **chomped** the sandwiches.

e)  Eleanna **ran** / **sprinted** to the door.

f)  Helena **throttled** / **squeezed** the bottle top in anger.

g)  Alan **shouted** / **screeched** at his neighbour.

h)  Liam **laughed** / **chortled** quietly to himself.

i)  Helen **breathed** / **gasped** quickly.

j)  Josh **scribbled** / **wrote** all over the paper.

## Making Verbs from Nouns

Work out the verb from the noun given.
**Example – Performance** is a noun. **Perform** is a verb.

a)  Explosion is a noun. _____ is a verb.

b)  Division is a noun. _____ is a verb.

c)  Departure is a noun. _____ is a verb.

d)  Hatred is a noun. _____ is a verb.

e)  Disturbance is a noun. _____ is a verb.

f)  Satisfaction is a noun. _____ is a verb.

g)  Arrival is a noun. _____ is a verb.

h)  Action is a noun. _____ is a verb.

i)  Proof is a noun. _____ is a verb.

j)  Invasion is a noun. _____ is a verb.

## More Verbs

**1** Draw lines between the boxes to match each description to the correct set of verbs.

| Description | Verbs |
|---|---|
| **a)** At a football match | Harvest, drive, sow |
| **b)** In a place of worship | Write, chat, answer |
| **c)** A cow in a field | Saw, hammer, cut |
| **d)** On a farm | Sweat, jump, sing |
| **e)** Children on the beach | Eat, cook, dine |
| **f)** Children in a lesson at school | Shoot, score, cheer |
| **g)** In a carpenter's shop | Prepare, bake, taste |
| **h)** In a shop | Pray, worship, kneel |
| **i)** At a rock concert | Buy, exchange, browse |
| **j)** In a restaurant | Chew, wander, moo |
| **k)** Cooking a meal | Dig, play, splash |

**2** Give two verbs of your own that could be used to write about each of the following:

**a)** At a football match    i) _____    ii) _____

**b)** In a place of worship    i) _____    ii) _____

**c)** A cow in a field    i) _____    ii) _____

**d)** On a farm    i) _____    ii) _____

**e)** Children on the beach    i) _____    ii) _____

**f)** Children in a lesson at school    i) _____    ii) _____

**g)** In a carpenter's shop    i) _____    ii) _____

**h)** In a shop    i) _____    ii) _____

**i)** At a rock concert    i) _____    ii) _____

**j)** In a restaurant    i) _____    ii) _____

**k)** Cooking a meal    i) _____    ii) _____

## Adverbs

For each of the following verbs, think of three adverbs that describe how the action might be done. The first one has been done for you.

| Verb | Adverb 1 | Adverb 2 | Adverb 3 |
|---|---|---|---|
| Walking | lazily | unsteadily | quickly |
| Eating | | | |
| Laughing | | | |
| Dancing | | | |
| Sleeping | | | |
| Playing football | | | |
| Cooking | | | |
| Fighting | | | |
| Talking | | | |

## Forming Adverbs

Using the rules below, look at the adjectives in the table and write down…
• the adverb you can make from them
• which rule to use to change adjectives into adverbs.

| | | |
|---|---|---|
| **Rule 1** – Change 'y' to 'i' and add 'ly', e.g. hearty – heartily | **Rule 2** – Drop 'e' before adding 'y', e.g. noble – nobly | **Rule 3** – Add 'ly', e.g. glad – gladly |

| Adjective | Adverb | Rule | Adjective | Adverb | Rule |
|---|---|---|---|---|---|
| Clever | | | Happy | | |
| Hungry | | | Poor | | |
| Sensible | | | Anxious | | |
| Idle | | | Probable | | |
| Brutal | | | Equal | | |

## Positioning Adverbs

An adverb has been given for each of the following sentences.
Rewrite each sentence three times, putting the adverb in a different place for each one.
Look at the example to help you.

**Example**
The boys left the room **sneakily**.
The boys **sneakily** left the room.

a) The castaways waved to the helicopter **desperately**.

i) ...................................................................................................................................

ii) ...................................................................................................................................

iii) ...................................................................................................................................

b) The fox crept through the garden **slyly**.

i) ...................................................................................................................................

ii) ...................................................................................................................................

iii) ...................................................................................................................................

c) The rain spread over the entire area **rapidly**.

i) ...................................................................................................................................

ii) ...................................................................................................................................

iii) ...................................................................................................................................

d) Jane began to make her speech **nervously**.

i) ...................................................................................................................................

ii) ...................................................................................................................................

iii) ...................................................................................................................................

e) David tripped over the rug **clumsily**.

i) ...................................................................................................................................

ii) ...................................................................................................................................

iii) ...................................................................................................................................

f) The man ran across the road **quickly**.

i) ...................................................................................................................................

ii) ...................................................................................................................................

iii) ...................................................................................................................................

# Forms of Persuasion

## Persuasion

Choose the correct technique from the options given to complete the following table.

**Threats and blackmail**　　**Flattery**　　**Statistics**　　**Rhetorical questions**

**Empathy**　　**Shock tactics**　　**Twisting arguments to support your views**

**Gaining sympathy / sob stories / guilt**　　**Rule of three**　　**Repetition**

**Making deals / compromise**　　**Emotive words**

| Persuasive technique | Persuasive example |
|---|---|
| a) | You must surely understand things from my point of view… |
| b) | Help me – it's my job at stake! |
| c) | If you really think you're that clever, why don't you prove it by helping me? |
| d) | My poor, sad, downtrodden family need help. |
| e) | I'm not asking for help, I'm not asking for advice – I just want a fair deal. |
| f) | A sensible, well-balanced person like you… |
| g) | Help me or I'll send the boys round. |
| h) | I have no money, home or friends, so surely you'd help me… |
| i) | Surely you can help me? |
| j) | Please, please, please help! |
| k) | If you help me, I'll help you. |
| l) | 99% of schoolchildren can't be wrong. |

## Emotive Words

Read the letter extract below and identify 10 emotive words that are used to try to persuade the reader.

> A generous, sensitive person like you should surely appreciate my terrible plight. I've desperately wanted to go to the Glastonbury festival for years. My heartless, uncaring parents never gave me enough money to achieve my dream. I'm hoping that with your considerate support and warm friendship I can make my yearning ambition a wonderful reality.

a) ...........................................  b) ...........................................  c) ...........................................

d) ...........................................  e) ...........................................  f) ...........................................

g) ...........................................  h) ...........................................  i) ...........................................

j) ...........................................

## Using Emotive Words

Using the emotive words you found above, write 10 sentences of your own to persuade someone.

a) ...........................................................................................................................

b) ...........................................................................................................................

c) ...........................................................................................................................

d) ...........................................................................................................................

e) ...........................................................................................................................

f) ...........................................................................................................................

g) ...........................................................................................................................

h) ...........................................................................................................................

i) ...........................................................................................................................

j) ...........................................................................................................................

## Using Persuasive Techniques

Say whether the following persuasive techniques are appropriate or inappropriate for their purpose and audience.

**a)** An educationalist persuading an examination board – 98% of children suffer from stress before exams, so the amount of exams should be reduced.

**b)** Persuading someone to help you after an accident – Please, please, please help me!

**c)** Trying to seriously persuade the bank to give you a loan – Can't you see the way I'm cruelly, desperately suffering?

**d)** A bailiff persuading someone to pay outstanding debts – Pay up, or we'll confiscate your TV.

**e)** A market stallholder trying to sell an item of clothing – I'm not asking £10, I'm not asking £5. All I want is £2.50.

**f)** A child trying to persuade their parents – If I wash the car, will I be allowed some pocket money?

**g)** Persuading a teacher – Why should we do homework? You might be captured by aliens before you get the chance to mark it.

**h)** Persuading an MP – A sensible, educated man like you would surely see my point.

**i)** Trying to stop a friend from embarrassing you – If you embarrass me, I'll post those embarrassing pictures of you on the internet!

**j)** Trying to persuade a friend to lend you money – Pretty, pretty please lend me £5.

**k)** Persuading someone to donate to charity – Give us some money now.

**l)** Persuading a close relative to sponsor you – Someone so close and dear to me would surely like to sponsor what I'm doing.

Letts and LONSDALE

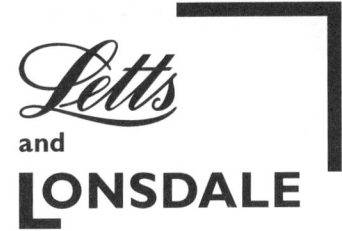

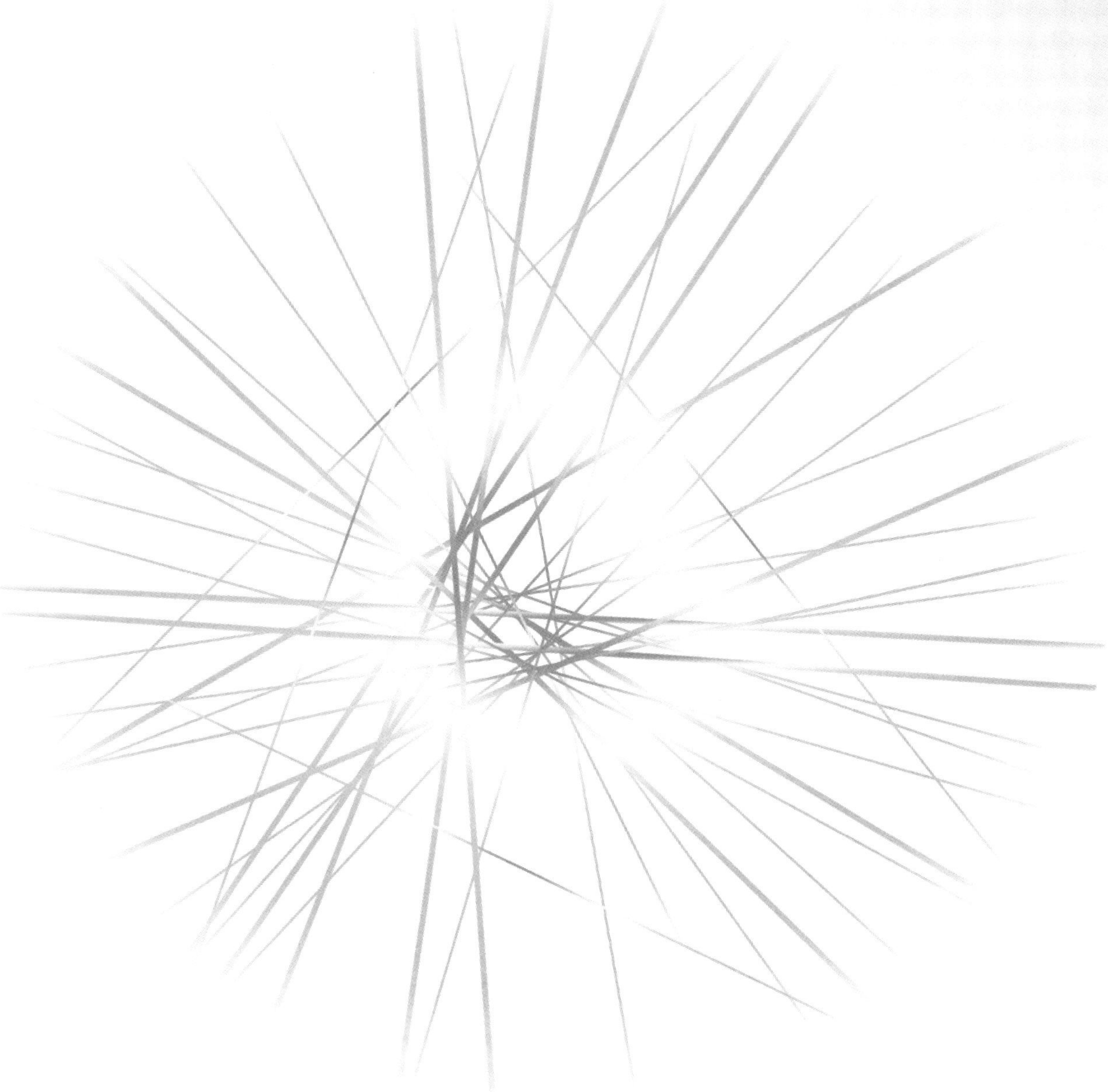

# ESSENTIALS

## Year 7
## KS3 English
Workbook Answers

Year 7 • KS3 English Workbook Answers

# PERSONAL WRITING

## Page 4–7

### Personal Profiles

| Feature | Yes | No |
|---|---|---|
| Slang | ✔ | |
| A large mixture of simple, compound and complex sentences | | ✔ |
| Personal opinions | ✔ | |
| Varied paragraphs | | ✔ |
| Headings | ✔ | |
| Lists | ✔ | |
| Use of first person | ✔ | |
| Asides to give extra information | ✔ | |

### Personal Writing 1

a) Sometimes true

b) True

c) False

d) False

e) Sometimes true

f) Sometimes true

g) Sometimes true

h) False

i) True

j) Sometimes true

k) False

l) True

m) False

### Personal Writing 2

1. a) social networking; promote

   b) programmes; magazines

   c) blog; diary

   d) audience

   e) journal; formal

   f) autobiography; exaggerate

2. Personal opinion - I couldn't be bothered with anything today.

   Slang - Everyone got on my wick.

   Emotive language - I desperately wanted to go out.

   Anecdote - It's like the time that I wanted to go to the zoo.

   Exaggeration - It's happened millions and millions of times before.

### Types of Personal Writing

| D | D | W | M | A | M | Y | F | O | R | O | I | G |
|---|---|---|---|---|---|---|---|---|---|---|---|---|
| I | V | S | T | O | R | Y | M | N | L | U | K | I |
| A | E | C | F | K | L | S | R | I | O | M | E | M |
| R | U | E | E | P | D | E | O | N | G | D | S | K |
| Y | T | S | J | R | J | N | J | B | B | M | Y | I |
| E | D | I | T | O | R | I | A | L | O | E | O | T |
| F | I | U | G | F | U | U | P | O | O | D | N | L |
| A | B | Q | K | I | X | R | O | G | K | N | R | P |
| L | N | R | H | L | B | E | N | A | E | F | E | O |
| S | B | K | S | E | Y | I | Z | A | P | I | K | E |
| S | T | A | T | E | M | E | N | T | L | E | M | T |
| R | C | O | M | A | B | R | N | S | E | Y | S | R |
| A | U | T | O | B | I | O | G | R | A | P | H | Y |

a) Diary

b) Editorial

c) Profile

d) Journal

e) Blog

f) Statement

g) Autobiography

h) Poetry

i) Story

j) Memoir

k) Log book

# SHAKESPEARE

## Page 8–11

### Shakespeare's Life

**a)–j)** William Shakespeare was born in Stoke-on-Trent (**Stratford-upon-Avon**) in Warwickshire in 1564. His mother was the daughter of a well-off landowner and his father was involved in the glove-making trade. Shakespeare probably went to the comprehensive (**Grammar**) school in Stratford-upon-Avon.

The next event in his life we can be certain of was his divorce (**marriage**) in 1582 to a farmer's daughter, Anne Hathaway. They had a baby girl in 1583 and triplets (**twins**) in 1585, two years after their first child. After this time, there are virtually no records of what happened in his life - these are often called his 'lost' years. The next recorded mention of him is in 1592, when he is documented as being a theatre worker.

As an actor, Shakespeare was connected to the Lord Playwright's (**Chamberlain's**) Company. This changed its name in 1603 to the King's when King Albert (**James**) came to the throne. The Company was financially involved in two theatres in Tottenham (**Southwark**), both of which were near to the river Thames. These theatres were called the Globe and the Blackfriars.

Although Shakespeare is mainly famous for his plays, it was his poetry that was published first, in 1593 and 1594. A large number of Shakespeare's novels (**plays**) were presumably written around this time too – the first written evidence of plays by Shakespeare occurs in 1594 and from then until 1611 he seemed to write about two plays a year. Among the first plays he wrote are *Titus Andronicus* and *A Midsummer Night's Dream*. In the early 1600s he started to write more comedies (**tragedies**) such as *Hamlet*, *King Lear* and *Othello*. From 1608 onwards, his later plays such as *Cymbeline* and *The Tempest* seem to have been written.

At the end of his life he returned to Stratford having made his fortune. He died on his birthday, 23rd April, in 1616. On his tomb in Holy Trinity Church, Burslem (**Stratford-upon-Avon**), there is a rhyme threatening to curse anyone who disturbs his bones! 7 years after his death in 1623 the first collected edition of his works was published.

### Shakespeare's Theatre

a) It was rebuilt using timber from an earlier theatre.

b) It burned down.

c) Its whereabouts remained unknown for over 300 years, until its foundations were discovered beneath a car park.

d) The buildings above it are listed (protected by law).

e) Different sources of evidence suggest it was either round or an 18/20-sided polygon.

f) The Puritans.

g) The Burbage family.

### Modern Meanings

a) Star-cross'd

b) Households

c) Civil blood

d) Toil

e) Misadventured

f) Attend

g) Ancient grudge

h) Continuance

i) New mutiny

j) Fatal loins

k) Nought

l) Strife

m) Traffic

### Shakespeare's Vocabulary

a) Things are often not as good as they appear to be.

b) Having lots of fun.

c) Innocent.

d) All at once.

e) Women are unreliable.

f) Bad deeds.

g) I haven't slept at all.

h) I have been really lucky.

i) I want fair revenge or compensation.

j) Saved at the last minute from a terrible fate.

## GENRE & SCIENCE FICTION

**Page 12–15**

**Science Fiction**

a)–e) **Any 5 suitable reasons, e.g.** The story is about time travel; It uses scientific vocabulary; It asks the question 'What if?'; It discusses scientific ideas; It talks about space.

**Written Genres**

a) Horror

b) Cowboy

c) Action adventure

d) Science fiction

e) Crime

f) History

g) Biography

h) Romance

i) Fantasy

j) Humour

**Identifying Genres**

a) i) Cowboy fiction

   ii) **Any 3 suitable reasons, e.g.** Set in wide open spaces; Cowboy language (Stetsons / canyon); Content includes horses, wind and other Western clichés.

b) i) Science fiction

   ii) **Any 3 suitable reasons, e.g.** Scientific language; Set in space; Content refers to technology; It is mysterious and asks, 'What if?'

**Identifying Genre from Vocabulary**

a) Crime

b) Fairy tale

c) Romance

d) History

e) Fantasy

f) Science fiction

g) Cowboy / Western

# THE WRITER'S CRAFT

**Page 16–19**

**Similes**

a) Fox

b) Mouse

c) Lead

d) Rake

e) Post

f) Church mouse

g) Lion

h) Lightning

i) Kitten

j) Hippo

k) Two peas in a pod

l) Fiddle

m) Bird

n) Lamb

o) Mustard

p) Hatter

q) Fruitcake

r) Houses

s) Rock

t) Old boots

**Adjectives, Metaphors & Similes**

1.  a) dirty; old; fabulous; new; sugar

    b) amazing

    c) little; exciting; immense

    d) French; unlucky; new

    e) old; immaculate; vast

2.  a) Simile – like lightning

    b) Metaphor – a cloud of gloom

    c) Simile – as depressed as a deflated balloon

    d) Metaphor – was a sweet treat

    e) Simile – looked like he had swallowed his false teeth

3.  a) forgetful

    b) hyperactive

**Descriptive Techniques 1**

a) Shiny; Crashing; Clinking; Dull; Depressed; Bad; Sad; Depressing; Rubber (gloves); Kitchen (stool)

b) Crashing, clinking; Depressed drumbeat; Depressing day

c) Splash; Thud; Crashing; Clinking; Crashed

d) Dull thud; Bad, sad

e) The kitchen stool rocked back on its heels

f) The sky cried

g) Sank like a stone

h) The dull thud of her footsteps was a depressed drumbeat of gloom; The kitchen stool rocked on its heels; The sky cried

**Descriptive Techniques 2**

a) Alliteration

b) Onomatopoeia

c) Personification

d) Pathetic fallacy

e) Adjectives

f) Simile

g) Metaphor

h) Onomatopoeia and simile

i) Assonance and alliteration

j) Alliteration

k) Metaphor

l) Adjectives

m) Adjectives

n) Alliteration

# MORE WRITER'S CRAFT

**Page 20–23**

**Verbs**

a) strolled

b) hammered

c) collapsed

d) chomped

e) sprinted

f) throttled

g) screeched

h) chortled

i) gasped

j) scribbled

**Making Verbs from Nouns**

a) Explode

b) Divide

c) Depart

d) Hate

e) Disturb

f) Satisfy

g) Arrive

h) Act

i) Prove

j) Invade

**More Verbs**

1. a) Shoot, score, cheer

   b) Pray, worship, kneel

   c) Chew, wander, moo

   d) Harvest, drive, sow

   e) Dig, play, splash

   f) Write, chat, answer

   g) Saw, hammer, cut

   h) Buy, exchange, browse

   i) Sweat, jump, sing

   j) Eat, cook, dine

   k) Prepare, bake, taste

2. a)-k) There are no right or wrong answers for this exercise, but you need to pick verbs that are mainly used in each place to give good answers.

**Adverbs**

There are no right or wrong answers for this exercise, but good answers will make complete sense for each verb.

**Forming Adverbs**

| Adjective | Adverb | Rule |
|-----------|--------|------|
| Clever | Cleverly | 3 |
| Hungry | Hungrily | 1 |
| Sensible | Sensibly | 2 |
| Idle | Idly | 2 |
| Brutal | Brutally | 3 |
| Happy | Happily | 1 |
| Poor | Poorly | 3 |
| Anxious | Anxiously | 3 |
| Probable | Probably | 2 |
| Equal | Equally | 3 |

**Positioning Adverbs**

a) **Desperately**, the castaways waved to the helicopter.

   The castaways **desperately** waved to the helicopter.

   The castaways waved **desperately** to the helicopter.

b) **Slyly**, the fox crept through the garden.

   The fox **slyly** crept through the garden.

   The fox crept **slyly** through the garden.

c) **Rapidly**, the rain spread over the entire area.

   The rain **rapidly** spread over the entire area.

The rain spread **rapidly** over the entire area.

d) **Nervously**, Jane began to make her speech.

   Jane **nervously** began to make her speech.

   Jane began to **nervously** make her speech.

e) David **clumsily** tripped over the rug.

   David tripped **clumsily** over the rug.

   **Clumsily**, David tripped over the rug.

f) The man **quickly** ran across the road.

   The man ran **quickly** across the road.

   **Quickly**, the man ran across the road.

# FORMS OF PERSUASION

**Page 24–27**

**Persuasion**

a) Empathy

b) Shock tactics

c) Twisting arguments so that they support your views

d) Emotive words

e) Rule of three

f) Flattery

g) Threats and blackmail

h) Gaining sympathy / sob stories / guilt

i) Rhetorical questions

j) Repetition

k) Making deals / compromise

l) Statistics

**Emotive Words**

a)-j) **In any order:** Generous; Sensitive; Terrible plight; Desperately; Heartless; Uncaring; Considerate; Yearning; Wonderful; Warm Friendship.

**Using Emotive Words**

There are no right or wrong answers for this exercise – the skill is in making informed choices about your writing. To write a good, persuasive sentence you will need to think about whether the persuasion needs to be formal or informal and base this on who you're trying to persuade. You will need to use a range of techniques and think about the order they can be placed in for maximum impact.

**Using Persuasive Techniques**

a) Appropriate

b) Appropriate

c) Inappropriate

d) Appropriate

e) Appropriate

**f)** Appropriate

**g)** Inappropriate

**h)** Appropriate

**i)** Inappropriate

**j)** Appropriate

**k)** Inappropriate

**l)** Appropriate

### Writing Appropriate Forms of Persuasion

**a)–l)** Appropriate responses consider the view of the person on the receiving end of the persuasive technique. If the sentence would persuade an average person in the circumstances described, using common sense, then the answers are appropriate.

# PUNCTUATION

## Page 28–31

### Commas and Full Stops

**a)** Whitney was loud, but Brittany was louder.

**b)** Callum liked football. Steven liked baseball.

**c)** Bethany swam for the county, although she wasn't fit.

**d)** Charlotte mumbled. Megan shouted.

**e)** Melanie did her homework, although she didn't want to.

**f)** Sarah smiled with delight. Sam frowned with disappointment.

**g)** James fidgeted in his seat, despite sitting on a cushion.

**h)** Anthony shouted at Ryan, which made Ryan angry.

**i)** Arlen got into trouble. He hadn't done his lines for the teacher.

**j)** Tom redid his homework, because he'd spilled his drink on it.

### Commas

**a)** The police arrested the man, which made the public very happy.

**b)** The girls bought dresses, shoes, make-up and chocolate.

**c)** Before he went to the match, Richard played his guitar.

**d)** After the holidays, the children had to go back to school.

**e)** Finally, the music stopped.

**f)** Because he had revised well, Sam passed the exam.

**g)** Cheese, peas, pickles and bananas do not make a good mixture.

**h)** Helen, after thinking about what she was going to do, decided to stay in.

**i)** Robbie wanted to go to England, but Donna didn't.

**j)** Everyone bought season tickets, scarves and replica shirts when their team got promoted.

**k)** Eventually, the book was finished.

### Colons and Semi-Colons

**1. a)** I could only find three of the ingredients: sausage, Cajun spice and rice.

**b)** To sum up: every time I eat vegetables it makes me think of you.

**c)** As a famous man once said: 'It's not what you do, it's how well you do it that counts.'

**d)** The pupils came back to school today; they had only been away for a few days.

**e)** The concert was made up of several parts including an overture; a middle section which went on for ages; a lengthy, boring second section; an interesting conclusion and a dull encore.

**2. a)–c)** Remember in your answers that a semi-colon is used to join two independent but related clauses that could be separate sentences.

**3. a)–c)** Remember in your answers that a colon is used to introduce a list of items, an explanation or a definition.

### Dashes and Hyphens

**a)** Hyphen

**b)** Dash

**c)** Dash first, then hyphen

**d)** Hyphen

**e)** Hyphen

### Apostrophes

| Sentence | Apostrophe of Omission | Apostrophe of Possession |
|---|---|---|
| The boys' football was confiscated by the teacher. | | ✔ |
| The boy's football was confiscated by the teacher. | | ✔ |
| The boy's going to get in trouble. | ✔ | |
| The teacher hadn't thought about how he would punish the boys | ✔ | |
| There wasn't any answer to the problem. | ✔ | |
| Can I borrow John's pen? | | ✔ |
| The girl's going home. | ✔ | |

### Inserting Apostrophes of Omission

**a)** Josh didn't want to do his Maths homework.

**b)** Whitney couldn't chew her toenails.

**c)** Hannah can't stand Harriet.

**d)** Tyler isn't a girl.

**e)** 'It's a frog!' shrieked Melanie.

**f)** 'I'll take the low road,' sang Alison.

**g)** 'You should've done your homework, Jess,' said Frank.

**h)** 'We've eaten all the pies,' said Matthew and Daniel.

**i)** 'No, you haven't,' replied Ryan.

**j)** 'I'm a teapot,' mumbled James.

**k)** 'You shouldn't have bought me anything,' replied his aunt.

**l)** 'We're promoted!' shouted the fans.

**m)** 'Why'd you do that? You've broken it now!' exclaimed Josh.

### Inserting Apostrophes of Possession

**a)** The children's work was featured at the exhibition.

**b)** Sir's hair was the shortest in the class.

**c)** 'You have copied Matthew's work!' said Miss.

**d)** **Any one from**: The film star's good looks were loved by all the girls (Stars is singular); The film stars' good looks, were loved by all the girls (Stars is plural).

**e)** **Any one from**: The result of the match shattered the fans' hopes (Fans is plural). The results of the match shattered the fan's hopes (Fans is singular).

**f)** The critic loved the band's new album.

**g)** Faye's brother was happy with his birthday present.

**h)** Lisa's job was only part-time.

**i)** Caroline was delighted by the play's success.

**j)** Rachel's new skirt was the talk of her school.

**k)** Lisa's persistent phone calls annoyed her friends.

**l)** Phil's skills as an organiser were in demand.

**m)** The boss questioned Craig's appointment.

### Common Confusions

**a)** There

**b)** It's

**c)** Hear

**d)** To

**e)** For

**f)** Their

**g)** Its

**h)** Here

**i)** Too; Too

**j)** Four

**k)** It's

**l)** You're

**m)** To; Two

# DRAMA TEXTS

## Page 32–35

### Drama Scripts

Remember that the whole script must link together and make sense – speeches must relate to what went before and what comes after.

### Stage Directions

**a)** Through his facial expression or body language.

**b)** **Any one from:** 'He wanders slowly DL'; 'Enter Robbie UR'; 'Peigi wanders UC and...'

**c)** (To himself)

**d)** (Aside to Peigi)

**e)** **Any one from:** 'He is wearing an orange t-shirt...'; '...picks up a leaflet from a rack...'

**f)** It is so the actors can find their speaking lines easier. However, some scripts have names in capitals in the stage directions too.

### Turning Prose into Drama

A good script will use all the advice given in the template on page 34.

### Stage Drama

**a)** An instruction for the actor / actress.

**b)** Speech said in a whisper by one character to another that others aren't supposed to hear.

**c)** Area in front of the proscenium arch.

**d)** Curtains.

**e)** The picture-frame shape of a traditional stage.

**f)** Part of the stage that sticks out in front of the proscenium arch and safety curtain.

**g)** Area in front of the stage where musicians sit.

**h)** A solo speech by one character on stage.

**i)** Sides of the stage where the performers wait and props are stored.

**j)** What happens when an actor starts laughing uncontrollably.

**k)** Curtain at the rear of the stage on which scenes are sometimes painted.

**l)** Towards the audience.

**m)** Away from the audience.

**n)** Items used in the performance.

**o)** A stage curtain rail.

**p)** Headphones.

**q)** Conversation between two or more characters.

**r)** The middle of the stage furthest from the audience.

**s)** The middle of the stage closest to the audience.

# READING FOR MEANING

## Page 36–39

### Reading Facts and Opinions

**a)** Opinion

**b)** Fact

**c)** Fact

**d)** Fact

**e)** Opinion

**f)** Fact

**g)** Fact

**h)** Opinion

**i)** Opinion

**j)** Opinion

## Facts and Opinions in Newspapers

| Newspaper Feature | Mainly Factual | Mainly Opinion |
|---|---|---|
| Letters to the Editor | | ✔ |
| Restaurant review | | ✔ |
| Sports scores | ✔ | |
| Weather prediction | | ✔ |
| Birth announcements | ✔ | |
| Rainfall measurements | ✔ | |
| Advice columns | | ✔ |
| Horoscopes | | ✔ |

## Finding Facts and Opinions

| Section | Fact | Opinion |
|---|---|---|
| I get on the Red Line Train | ✔ | |
| Avant-garde Millenium Park | | ✔ |
| The gorgeous interior | | ✔ |
| Hear a free lunchtime concert | ✔ | |
| Head due north to Wrigley Field | ✔ | |
| There's nowhere in the city that beats an afternoon spent here | | ✔ |
| Nothing heals the soul quite like ice cream | | ✔ |
| Makes its own chocolates and hot fudge on the premises | ✔ | |
| Oddball accessories | | ✔ |
| Two venues nearby offer bands just about nightly | ✔ | |

## Reading for Purpose

1. **a)** Instruments used in rock music – Guitar; Bass; Drums; Keyboards (e.g. Organ; Piano; Synthesizer)

   Other instruments sometimes used – Harmonica; Stringed instruments (e.g. Violin; Cello); Flute; Banjo; Mandolin; Horns (e.g. Trumpets; Trombones); Sitar

   **b)** Rock music was influenced by – Blues; R&B; Country; Gospel; Contemporary pop; Jazz; Folk. It was also later influenced by Soul, Funk, and Latin music.
   Rock music has influenced – Folk-rock; Blues-rock; Psychedelic rock; Soft rock; Heavy metal; Hard rock; Progressive rock; Punk rock; Synth-rock; Hardcore punk; Alternative rock; Grunge; Britpop; Indie rock; Nu-metal.

   **c)** Strong, insistent, repetitive beat; Up-tempo; Lively; Memorable tunes.

2. Your paragraphs should pick out all the relevant information from question 1. They should be placed in a logical order with the information in relevant groups (for example, all the information about the instruments used in rock music placed in the same paragraph) so that it makes complete sense.

## Types of Reading

1. **a)** Skim

   **b)** Intensive

   **c)** Scan

   **d)** Extensive

   **e)** Intensive

   **f)** Intensive

   **g)** Intensive

   **h)** Extensive

   **i)** Scan

   **j)** Intensive

2. **Any three from:** Constant gigging; Treating the band seriously; Radio exposure; Winning a European award; Multi-tasking; versatile band members.

# WRITING FOR AN AUDIENCE

**Page 40–43**

### Non-Fiction Writing

**a)** Any mention of the dates in the extract.

**b)** Any reference to a person's name or he / his / she / it etc e.g. 'her new husband.'

**c)** Any mention of facts or dates, e.g. 'Doreen was 21 soon to be 22 on August 15.'

**d)** Any mention of names, e.g. '…his mother, formerly Doreen Hughes.'

**e)** Any of the information about Ian Curtis' family.

**f)** Any sentences that contain careful wording like 'probably' or straightforward factual comment.

**g)** Any example, e.g. 'had met.'

### Features of a Review

**a)** more than a tasty gumbo of spicy ingredients

**b)** marvellous motion picture moments

**c)** Ratatouille is brilliant – go and see it.

**d)** a possibly yucky story

**e)** boy his toy

**f)** I could be boring you with my gushing about this film, but it's a risk I'm prepared to take

**g)** Brad Bird, director of The Incredibles

**h)** Much like the feel of Christmas film 'It's a Wonderful Life'

### Instructions

**1.** A5; B4; C2; D1; E6; F3

**2.** Use Question 1 as an example of how to make a list of instructions.

### Newspaper Features

**a)** name

**b)** columns

**c)** caption

**d)** headline

**e)** teaser

**f)** puns

**g)** banner

**h)** contents

**i)** gossip

**j)** editorial

**k)** broadsheet

**l)** sports

**m)** cartoon

**n)** bold

**o)** lead

**p)** scoop

**q)** beginning

## WRITING FAIRY TALES

### Page 44–47

### Creative Writing

**a–c)** There are many different ways these sentences can be written. A good answer will create a consistent mood or style that the reader will recognise.

### Planning a Story

**a–d)** This question is testing your skills of organisation, so there isn't a right or wrong way to do this, but your ideas should make sense and have a logical order.

### Planning the Parts of a Story

**a)** Denouement

**b)** Anti-climax

**c)** Crisis

**d)** Conclusion

**e)** Resolution

**f)** Climax

**g)** Introduction

**h)** Rising action

**i)** Falling action

**j)** Twist

### Planning the Sequence of a Story

A good answer will put the parts of the story in an order that keeps the reader's interest and varies the overall tone and pace.

### Improving your Draft

This exercise is to make you think about why you should include certain words and for what effect, a skill that writers need at all levels. The way to tell whether your version is better than the original is to read the two versions to someone and see how they react.

## MEDIA TEXTS

### Page 48–51

### The Language of Text Messages

**1. a)** Hello. Are you coming to see me? I have had a new haircut… oh dear! It's bad. (LOL = Laugh out loud, but it's often just used for emphasis, as it is here).

   **b)** Are you mad? I'm rolling on the floor with laughter – in my opinion you are very silly.

**2. a–b)** Remember to abbreviate words and use numbers to make sounds, for example '8' for 'ate' or 'eight' sounds. There are different ways that you might do this but a good answer will sound like the original message when read out loud.

### The Language of Email

**a)** True

**b)** True

**c)** False

**d)** False

**e)** False

### Newspapers and Magazines

**a)** Specialist music magazine

**b)** Technology magazine

**c)** Home and cooking magazines

**d)** A fanzine for a band

**e)** A free local newspaper

**f)** Chart music magazine

**g)** Broadsheet newspaper

**h)** TV guide

**i)** Gossip magazine

**j)** Tabloid newspaper

**Research**

If you think a newspaper or magazine is aimed at a varied audience, then include the different types of people you think it's aimed at. This exercise is designed to make you think about who newspapers and magazines are aimed at and there are no definite right or wrong answers. If you can give reasons as to why you think it is aimed at a particular type of reader, then it is a good answer.

**Advertising**

A4; B6; C7; D2; E3; F1; G8; H5

**Media Language**

A5; B12; C6; D1; E4; F2; G3; H10; I8; J9; K11; L7

---

**How to judge your level from this book – a general guide.**

**At level 4 or below** – you will be getting **some** of the exercises right, but you may have gaps in your knowledge. To improve, you will need to revisit those areas you do not understand and work your way carefully through them.

**At level 5** – you should be **getting over half the exercises fully right** and you will be **getting at least a few things right in most exercises**. To improve, you will need to focus on your area of weakness and look at the things you got wrong and why.

**At level 6** – you should be **getting a lot of things right in most exercises**. You will have **very few exercises where you didn't get at least half the answers right** or more. To improve, again you will need to see which parts of the exercises were not done quite so well and look at how to improve them.

**At level 7** – you will be **getting nearly everything right on nearly all the exercises**. Look at where you can improve and see if you can use the things you have learnt in unusual, striking and effective ways.

---

**ACKNOWLEDGEMENTS**

The author and publisher are grateful to the copyright holders for permission to use quoted materials and images.

Every effort has been made to trace copyright holders and obtain their permission for the use of copyright material. The authors and publishers will gladly receive information enabling them to rectify any error or omission in subsequent editions. All facts are correct at time of going to press.

Letts and Lonsdale
4 Grosvenor Place
London SW1X 7DL

School orders:                        015395 64910
School enquiries:                     015395 65921
Parent and student enquiries:   015395 64913
Email:     enquiries@lettsandlonsdale.co.uk
Websites: www.lettsandlonsdale.com

**ISBN: 978-1-905896-68-4**

01/300508

Published by Letts and Lonsdale

© 2008 Lonsdale, a division of Huveaux Plc.

British Library Cataloguing in Publication Data.

A CIP record of this book is available from the British Library.

**Book concept and development:** Helen Jacobs and Rebecca Skinner
**Author:** Nicolas Barber
**Project Editor:** Robert Dean
**Cover Design:** Angela English
**Inside Concept Design:** Helen Jacobs and Sarah Duxbury
**Text Design and Layout:** Little Red Dog
**Artwork:** Letts and Lonsdale

Printed and bound in Italy.

Letts and Lonsdale make every effort to ensure that all paper used in our books is made from wood pulp obtained from well-managed forests.

## Writing Appropriate Forms of Persuasion

Write sentences of your own in which you use the given form of persuasion in an appropriate manner.

To give good, appropriate answers, consider how the person who is being persuaded might feel and respond.

a) Use flattery to get a refund from a shop.

b) Make a parent feel guilty to get them to allow you to go to a party.

c) Use a rhetorical question to get a friend to agree with your point of view.

d) Use statistics to persuade a company to stop making a harmful product.

e) Use repetition to persuade a friend to help you do your homework.

f) Use empathy to persuade readers of a leaflet to donate to less well-off people.

g) Use shock tactics to persuade someone to stop smoking.

h) Twist a friend's argument to get them to agree to go with you to watch a film they say they don't like.

i) Use emotive words to get someone to donate to charity.

j) Use the rule of three to persuade a friend that you want them to go on holiday with you.

k) Use blackmail to make a friend stop gossiping about you.

l) Make a deal with a parent in order to get them to let you have a sleepover with friends.

# Punctuation

## Commas and Full Stops

Insert the correct punctuation in the following sentences, placing either a full stop or comma where it is marked with an asterisk.

a) Whitney was loud * but Brittany was louder.

b) Callum liked football * Steven liked baseball.

c) Bethany swam for the county * although she wasn't fit.

d) Charlotte mumbled * Megan shouted.

e) Melanie did her homework * although she didn't want to.

f) Sarah smiled with delight * Sam frowned with disappointment.

g) James fidgeted in his seat * despite sitting on a cushion.

h) Anthony shouted at Ryan * which made Ryan angry.

i) Arlen got into trouble * he hadn't done his lines for the teacher.

j) Tom redid his homework * because he'd spilled his drink on it.

## Commas

The following sentences have commas missing from them. Where should they go?

a) The police arrested the man which made the public very happy.

b) The girls bought dresses shoes make-up and chocolate.

c) Before he went to the match Richard played his guitar.

d) After the holidays the children had to go back to school.

e) Finally the music stopped.

f) Because he had revised well Sam passed the exam.

g) Cheese peas pickles and bananas do not make a good mixture.

h) Helen after thinking about what she was going to do decided to stay in.

i) Robbie wanted to go to England but Donna didn't.

j) Everyone bought season tickets scarves and replica shirts when their team got promoted.

k) Eventually the book was finished.

## Colons and Semi-Colons

**1** Insert either a semi-colon or a colon in the following sentences where it is marked with an asterisk.

   **a)** I could only find three of the ingredients * sausage, Cajun spice and rice.

   **b)** To sum up * every time I eat vegetables it makes me think of you.

   **c)** As a famous man once said * 'It's not what you do, it's how well you do it that counts.'

   **d)** The pupils came back to school today * they had only been away for a few days.

   **e)** The concert was made up of several parts including an overture * a middle section which went on for ages * a lengthy, boring second section * an interesting conclusion and a dull encore.

**2** Write three sentences of your own in which you use a semi-colon correctly.

   **a)**

   **b)**

   **c)**

**3** Write three sentences of your own in which you use a colon correctly.

   **a)**

   **b)**

   **c)**

## Dashes and Hyphens

Say whether there are hyphens or dashes in the following sentences.

**a)** The boy possessed no self-control.

**b)** There was a pause – then the room fell silent.

**c)** The group were influential – no-one had heard anything like them before.

**d)** The boxer was punch-drunk from the fight.

**e)** The well-known author recited his work very well.

## Apostrophes

Tick the boxes to say whether each sentence contains an apostrophe of omission or an apostrophe of possession.

| Sentence | Apostrophe of Omission | Apostrophe of Possession |
| --- | --- | --- |
| The boys' football was confiscated by the teacher. | | |
| The boy's football was confiscated by the teacher. | | |
| The boy's going to get in trouble. | | |
| The teacher hadn't thought about how he would punish the boys. | | |
| There wasn't any answer to the problem. | | |
| Can I borrow John's pen? | | |
| The girl's going home. | | |

## Inserting Apostrophes of Omission

Place apostrophes of omission in the correct places in the following sentences.

a) Josh didnt want to do his maths homework.

b) Whitney couldnt chew her toenails.

c) Hannah cant stand Harriet.

d) Tyler isnt a girl.

e) 'Its a frog!' shrieked Melanie.

f) 'Ill take the low road,' sang Alison.

g) 'You shouldve done your homework, Jess,' said Frank.

h) 'Weve eaten all the pies,' said Matthew and Daniel.

i) 'No, you havent,' replied Ryan.

j) 'Im a teapot,' mumbled James.

k) 'You shouldnt have bought me anything,' replied his aunt.

l) 'Were promoted,' shouted the fans.

m) 'Whyd you do that? Youve broken it now!' exclaimed Josh.

## Inserting Apostrophes of Possession

Place apostrophes of possession in the correct places in the following sentences.

a) The childrens work was featured at the exhibition.

b) Sirs hair was the shortest in the class.

c) 'You have copied Matthews work!' said Miss.

d) The film stars good looks were loved by all the girls.

e) The result of the match shattered the fans hopes.

f) The critics loved the bands new album.

g) Fayes brother was happy with his birthday present.

h) Lisas job was only part-time.

i) Caroline was delighted by the plays success.

j) Rachels new hairstyle was the talk of the school.

k) Lisas persistent phone calls annoyed her friends.

l) Phils skills as an organiser were in demand.

m) The boss questioned Craigs appointment.

## Common Confusions

Circle the correct option in the following sentences.

a) '**They're / Their / There** is no correct answer,' said the teacher.

b) **Its / it's** difficult to run a marathon.

c) **Here / Hear** what the opposition have to say before you make a decision.

d) 'Are you going **to / two / too** the cinema?' asked Laura.

e) 'What did you do that **four / for / fore?**' replied Mia.

f) 'Is that **they're / there / their** new car?' chuckled Liam.

g) 'Where is **its / it's** starter switch?' asked Philippa.

h) 'The entrance is over **here / hear!**' shouted Alex.

i) 'You've done **to / two / too** much **to / two / too** soon,' said David to Arthur.

j) 'There are **for / four / fore** reasons why you should visit Stoke, but none of them are to do with football!' said Tony.

k) '**Its / It's** not my fault,' moaned Lee.

l) '**You're / Your** the best person for the job,' said Bill.

m) 'I'm going **to / two / too** see the band on **to / two / too** separate occasions,' said Lily.

# Drama Texts

Below is one side of a telephone conversation. Finish the conversation to make it read like one of the following:

- Speaker 1 is arranging a date.
- Speaker 1 is planning a robbery.
- Speaker 1 has won the lottery.

Speaker 1: ...........................................................................................................

..................................................................................................................

Speaker 2: Pardon?

Speaker 1: ...........................................................................................................

..................................................................................................................

Speaker 2: You can't be serious!

Speaker 1: ...........................................................................................................

..................................................................................................................

Speaker 2: But what if I did that?

Speaker 1: ...........................................................................................................

..................................................................................................................

Speaker 2: But that's impossible!

Speaker 1: ...........................................................................................................

..................................................................................................................

Speaker 2: I suppose so...

Speaker 1: ...........................................................................................................

..................................................................................................................

Speaker 2: OK.

Speaker 1: ...........................................................................................................

..................................................................................................................

Speaker 2: I'll have a think about it.

Speaker 1: ...........................................................................................................

..................................................................................................................

Read the script extract and answer the questions that follow.

> DANIEL: (Looking puzzled) Is this the way to the concert?
> (He wanders slowly DL and scratches his head)
>
> PEIGI: Yes, I'm pretty sure it is, but they're not going to let you in. (She turns and sulks)
>
> DANIEL: Why not? I'm on the guest list!
> (Enter Robbie UR – he is wearing an orange t-shirt and bright red training shoes, which means that he is immediately noticed by Daniel and Peigi)
>
> PEIGI: Robbie! I didn't know you were coming this way. I thought I wouldn't see you until the concert tonight. (She smiles smugly and sneers at Daniel)
>
> ROBBIE: I'm just on my way to the soundcheck. (Aside to Peigi) Is that Dan?
> (He indicates DL)
>
> PEIGI: Sure is.
>
> ROBBIE: (To himself) I wish it wasn't... all he does is heckle me.
> (To Daniel) Oh, hi, Dan – good to see you...!
>
> (The two men shake hands. Robbie is clearly uncomfortable. Peigi wanders UC and picks up a leaflet from a rack upstage. She fans herself with the leaflet to imply that it is warm)

**a)** In the first line, how might the actor carry out the stage direction?

**b)** Write down one stage direction that tells the actor or actress where to stand on stage.

**c)** Write down one stage direction where only the audience are supposed to hear the words spoken and not the characters on stage.

**d)** Write down one stage direction where two of the actors are supposed to hear what is being said, but the other isn't.

**e)** Write down one stage direction that gives an idea of what props and scenery are needed on stage.

**f)** Why are the characters' names written in capitals at the start of their line, but not in their stage directions?

## Turning Prose into Drama

Using the storyline of a well-known fairy tale, e.g. Cinderella, plan and write the opening scene for a film script of the story in the template below. Think about the characters you need to write parts for.

| Description of opening scene. Where will it take place? What is on stage? What movements will the characters make? Include lighting stage directions to help create the mood. |
| --- |
|  |

| Names of characters (make them stand out). | Write speeches here; leave gaps between them. Use stage directions to indicate who the characters are talking to, to tell them how to say their lines and move, and for sound effects. |
| --- | --- |
|  |  |

## Stage Drama

Draw lines between the boxes to match the phrase used in drama and theatre with its meaning.

| Phrase | Meaning |
|--------|---------|
| **a)** Stage direction | Part of the stage that sticks out in front of the proscenium arch and safety curtain. |
| **b)** Aside | A solo speech by one character on stage. |
| **c)** Front of house | Sides of the stage where performers wait and props are often stored. |
| **d)** Tabs | Towards the audience. |
| **e)** Proscenium arch | Conversation between two or more characters. |
| **f)** Apron | Curtains. |
| **g)** Orchestra pit | The picture-frame shape of a traditional stage. |
| **h)** Soliloquy | An instruction for the actor / actress. |
| **i)** Wings | The middle of the stage closest to the audience. |
| **j)** Corpse | Area in front of the proscenium arch. |
| **k)** Back-cloth | What happens when an actor starts laughing uncontrollably. |
| **l)** Downstage | Speech said in a whisper by one character to another that others aren't supposed to hear. |
| **m)** Upstage | A stage curtain rail. |
| **n)** Properties | The middle of the stage furthest from the audience. |
| **o)** Banjo | Headphones |
| **p)** Cans | Curtain at the rear of the stage, on which scenes are sometimes painted. |
| **q)** Dialogue | Away from the audience. |
| **r)** UC | Items used in the performance. |
| **s)** DC | Area in front of the stage where musicians sit. |

# Reading for Meaning

## Reading Facts and Opinions

Say whether the following statements are fact or opinion.

**a)** Blue is the best colour. .....................................

**b)** Staffordshire is an English county. .....................................

**c)** All people must breathe to live. .....................................

**d)** Most people have two arms and two legs. .....................................

**e)** I don't like cabbage. .....................................

**f)** Wine is a drink. .....................................

**g)** Fire needs oxygen to burn. .....................................

**h)** He is silly. .....................................

**i)** Pizza tastes great. .....................................

**j)** Everyone loves football. .....................................

## Facts and Opinions in Newspapers

Here is a list of newspaper features.
Tick the boxes to say whether they are mainly factual or based more on opinion.

| Newspaper Feature | Mainly Factual | Mainly Opinion |
|---|---|---|
| Letters to the Editor | | |
| Restaurant review | | |
| Sports scores | | |
| Weather prediction | | |
| Birth announcements | | |
| Rainfall measurements | | |
| Advice columns | | |
| Horoscopes | | |

## Finding Facts and Opinions

Read the following passage. Decide whether the underlined sections are fact or opinion and tick the relevant box in the table below.

**A Top Day in Chicago**

I start the day in Chinatown, wandering from bakery to bakery while nibbling a coffee cream roll, chestnut cake and almond cookie in rapid succession, then shopping for staples like toast-scented Hello Kitty erasers and baseball-bat-shaped chopstick holders. <u>I get on the Red Line train</u> and alight downtown near <u>avant-garde Millennium Park</u>, stopping for a long time to admire 'The Bean' sculpture and to watch it reflect the city skyline. I follow up with a visit across the street to the Chicago Cultural Centre to gawk at <u>the gorgeous interior</u> and <u>hear a free lunchtime concert</u>.

Next, I hop back on the Red Line and <u>head due north to Wrigley Field</u> to catch a Cubs game. If the sun is shining and the breeze is blowing, <u>there's nowhere in the city that beats an afternoon spent here</u>; if the sun is obscured and the breeze blizzard-like, that sucks but at least tickets are easier to come by. I order a hot dog and Old Style beer and sigh as the Cubs get clobbered. <u>Nothing heals the soul quite like ice cream</u>, so it's off to Bucktown and Margies, an old-fashioned parlor that <u>makes its own chocolates and hot fudge on the premises</u>. I dawdle for a few hours around the little shops selling stylish clothing, <u>oddball accessories</u>, records and books in the Bucktown / Wicker Park neighbourhood, then consider where to go for the evening's live music finale. <u>Two venues nearby offer bands just about nightly</u>: Phyllis', a former Polish polka bar that now hosts scrappy up-and-coming bands, and the Hideout, hosting indie-oriented rock, folk and country musicians. I stop in for a set at the former, finish with a nightcap at the latter, then cab it home, convinced once again that Chicago is my kind of town.

By Karla Zimmerman, taken from the *Lonely Planet* website.

| Section | Fact | Opinion |
|---|---|---|
| I get on the Red Line Train | | |
| Avant-garde Millenium Park | | |
| The gorgeous interior | | |
| Head a free lunchtime concert | | |
| Head due north to Wrigley Field | | |
| There's nowhere in the city that beats an afternoon spent here | | |
| Nothing heals the soul quite like ice cream | | |
| Makes its own chocolates and hot fudge on the premises | | |
| Oddball accessories | | |
| Two venues nearby offer bands just about nightly | | |

## Reading for Purpose

**1** Read the following passage to identify…

**a)** the instruments used in rock music

**b)** other kinds of music that have influenced, or have been influenced by, rock music

**c)** what rock music sounds like.

Highlight the different types of information, using different colours for each one.

Rock music is a type of music with a strong vocal line backed by guitar, bass and drums. It usually has a strong beat and uses guitars (solid electric, hollow electric, or acoustic). Many other instruments are often used, including keyboard instruments (organ, piano and synthesizer), and harmonica, violin, flute, banjo, melodica, and timpani. Stringed instruments such as the mandolin and sitar are sometimes used, but to a lesser extent.

A rock band or rock group is a group of musicians who play rock music. Often, rock groups are made up of a guitarist, lead singer, bass guitarist, and drummer, forming a four-piece, or quartet. Some groups use a lead singer who can play an instrument while singing at the same time. Other groups include extra musicians, such as two guitarists to play rhythm and lead guitar, and a keyboardist. Occasionally, rock groups employ stringed instruments (e.g. violins, cellos), or horns (e.g. trumpets, trombones).

Rock and roll music consists of three chords and a strong, insistent, repetitive beat. The 1940s and 1950s saw the birth of rock and roll and rockabilly. Blues, R&B and country music merged with gospel, contemporary pop music, jazz and folk music. Along with a blues-music song structure, these influences formed a lively, up-tempo music that people could dance to with memorable tunes that stuck in the mind.

In the late 1960s, rock and folk music mixed to create folk-rock. Rock music also absorbed other types of music and created hybrids, such as with blues to create blues-rock, and with jazz to create jazz-rock fusion. Rock also developed in a very loose form to make psychedelic rock, in which time signatures were not as formulaic. The 1970s saw rock music become influenced by more unusual types of music, such as soul, funk, and Latin music. A number of subgenres (minor off-shoots), such as soft rock, heavy metal, hard rock, progressive rock, and punk rock, also developed. The 1980s saw further subgenres of rock music develop, including synth-rock, hardcore punk and alternative rock. Grunge, Britpop, indie rock, and nu-metal were rock subgenres that developed in the 1990s.

**2** Rewrite the information into three new paragraphs, including only the information you have picked out in question 1.

## Types of Reading

**1** Which type of reading would you use for each of the following?
Tick the correct option.

| Task | Skim | Scan | Extensive | Intensive |
|---|---|---|---|---|
| **a)** Looking at newspapers in a shop when deciding what to buy. | | | | |
| **b)** Reading the instructions for an exam. | | | | |
| **c)** Reading the TV guide in a magazine or newspaper in order to find out what's on tonight. | | | | |
| **d)** Reading *Pride and Prejudice* by Jane Austen for pleasure. | | | | |
| **e)** Reading a section of a contract. | | | | |
| **f)** Reading the instructions to work an item of electrical equipment. | | | | |
| **g)** Reading a website to find directions to a particular place. | | | | |
| **h)** Reading a biography for your own interest. | | | | |
| **i)** Reading a leaflet to find out where to go on a day out. | | | | |
| **j)** Reading an extract in a textbook to find the answers to a question or series of questions. | | | | |

**2** Read the following passage intensively and write down three ways in which Elvis Fontenot and the Sugar Bees have been successful in what they do.

Formed in 1993, Elvis Fontenot and the Sugar Bees have become well-known figures on the roots music scene because of their constant gigging. Despite having day jobs, the members treat the band as a full-time hobby, which they take very seriously. This has led to exposure on national radio and abroad, which in turn has led to further exposure and success. Winning a European music award in 2006 increased their profile worldwide. The members of the band are able to multi-task and play a variety of instruments, which makes them musically versatile.

a) ......................................................................................................

b) ......................................................................................................

c) ......................................................................................................

# Writing for an Audience

## Non-Fiction Writing

Read the biography extract and find an example of each of the features that follow.

> Ian Kevin Curtis was born into a close, loving, respectable, working class family on St. Swithin's Day - July 15 - in 1956. This is the day when legend has it that if it rains it will continue to do so for the next 40 days, or if it is fine then the sun will shine for a similar period. His mother remembers that it didn't rain. The place of birth was Basford House, a cottage hospital in Old Trafford that was popular among local pregnant mothers, especially the Peter Pan ward with its large stained glass windows and images of author J.M. Barrie's most famous creation, the boy who never grew up. The baby weighed in at 9lb 4oz, above average, but there were no birthing problems.
>
> Ian's parents had been married for almost four years when their first child was born. His mother, formerly Doreen Hughes, tied the knot with Kevin Curtis on August 9th, 1952. Doreen was 21, soon to be 22 on August 15, her new husband five years older. The service was held at St. John's Church in Old Trafford, the same church where Ian would be christened, and was followed by a reception at the Star cafe in Chorlton. Doreen had met Kevin on a blind date when she was 18, introduced by her friend Edna whose boyfriend worked alongside him in the railway police, as today's British Transport Police were then known. Edna had a photo of Doreen that was taken on an outing to Southport and had showed it to Kevin. Suitably impressed, he suggested a foursome to be arranged and they all went to the Imperial, a cinema in Brook's Bar, on the borders of Old Trafford and Chorlton. Doreen doesn't remember what film they saw.
>
> From *Torn Apart: The Life of Ian Curtis* by Mick Middles and Lindsay Reade.

**a)** Generally in chronological order

....................................................................................................................

**b)** Use of third person

....................................................................................................................

**c)** Use of facts and dates

....................................................................................................................

**d)** Use of names

....................................................................................................................

**e)** Background information to the main story to make the writer sound convincing

....................................................................................................................

**f)** Formal style

....................................................................................................................

**g)** Use of past tense

....................................................................................................................

## Features of a Review

Read the following film review. The underlined parts of the text are all key features of this review. Match them to features **a)–h)** below.

You probably wouldn't believe - or want to believe - <u>a possibly yucky story</u> involving food and rats, but that's what you get with this collection of <u>marvellous motion picture moments!</u> Remy the rat is obsessed with food; not just eating it, but cooking it too, and he goes to extreme lengths to make his dreams come true. He's obviously too small to do all the work himself, so he makes a kitchen <u>boy his toy</u> - but will the health inspector be injurious to his health and long-term dreams?

<u>Brad Bird, director of The Incredibles,</u> has hit another winner with this superbly constructed and delivered family movie. It works on so many levels - as a family film, as slapstick for the children and as thought-provoking set-pieces questioning our own way in life. <u>Much like the feel of Christmas favourite 'It's a Wonderful Life',</u> you'll feel sorry for the unlikely hero and wish that you had his appetite in pursuing your own dreams. The plot is <u>more than a tasty gumbo of spicy ingredients</u> – it works as one complete recipe, with excitement and humour alongside heartbreak and romance. What more could you want for the price of a cinema ticket?

<u>I could be boring you with my gushing about this film, but it's a risk I'm prepared to take</u> – it's simply that good. Match up a visit to your local cinema with a trip to a restaurant and you'll have a taste-filled stir-fry of a night! <u>Ratatouille is brilliant – go and see it.</u>

**a)** Pun based on the subject of the film.

**b)** Alliteration to make the review catchy.

**c)** Summary to let the reader know what is felt overall.

**d)** Use of slang to make the review seem informal.

**e)** Rhyme to make key points catchy.

**f)** Personal opinion.

**g)** Names and facts to add a serious formal note to the review.

**h)** Background references to help the reader compare the film to others.

## Instructions

**1** Instructions should be easy to follow, but these instructions about how to make a cup of tea are muddled. Number the instructions 1–8 to rearrange them into a logical order.

**A** Add milk. ☐

**B** Leave enough room to allow milk to be added. ☐

**C** Place a teabag and sugar in a cup, while waiting. ☐

**D** Put water in the kettle and boil. ☐

**E** Stir with a teaspoon and drink. ☐

**F** Pour boiling water into the cup. ☐

**2** Write your own set of instructions in a logical order. Try explaining how to tie a shoelace, in 10 steps or less. Remember to start most of your instructions with imperative verbs (i.e. Do, Don't, etc.).

a) ....................................................................................................

....................................................................................................

b) ....................................................................................................

....................................................................................................

c) ....................................................................................................

....................................................................................................

d) ....................................................................................................

....................................................................................................

e) ....................................................................................................

....................................................................................................

f) ....................................................................................................

....................................................................................................

g) ....................................................................................................

....................................................................................................

h) ....................................................................................................

....................................................................................................

i) ....................................................................................................

....................................................................................................

j) ....................................................................................................

## Newspaper Features

Choose the correct word from the options given to complete the sentences below.

bold    teaser    headline    columns    beginning    banner    contents    caption
editorial    scoop    broadsheet    puns    sports    name    lead    cartoon    gossip

**a)** The masthead is the _____ at the top of the front page.

**b)** A newspaper is usually set out in _____ .

**c)** Underneath a picture or photograph you will usually find a _____, which explains or comments on it.

**d)** A _____ is the quick guide to the main story on the front page.

**e)** A _____ article is one that gives you a few clues about the full article, but makes you want to read on, usually by buying the paper and reading inside.

**f)** Tabloid newspapers often use _____ to make their headings catchy.

**g)** A _____ is something that is long and narrow and usually goes across a page. It might include information, articles or adverts.

**h)** The front pages of many newspapers have a summary of the _____ inside.

**i)** Newspapers often contain many non-news items, like a TV guide, entertainment and _____ columns.

**j)** The _____ is the part where the newspaper's opinion is set out, with regard to the important issues of the day.

**k)** A _____ newspaper is generally seen as more serious and formal than a tabloid newspaper.

**l)** The back pages of newspapers are traditionally filled with _____ articles and stories.

**m)** Many newspapers use a _____ to visually comment on an important story or issue.

**n)** Headlines are put in _____ type to make them stand out.

**o)** The _____ story is the main story, usually on the cover of the paper.

**p)** An exclusive story that one newspaper has got that no other papers have is called a _____ .

**q)** The dateline is the line at the _____ of a news story that says where and when the story is from.

# Writing Fairy Tales

## Creative Writing

Different effects can be achieved with the same content, simply by changing the descriptive words in a passage. Below is a passage with all the descriptive words removed.

**a)** Insert frightening words to make it sound scary.

I walked ................................ through the ................................ garden. At both sides of me I saw ................................ plants and ................................ trees. I felt ................................ . In front of me was a ................................ building with a ................................ door. I knocked ................................ . The ................................ door ................................ opened and a ................................ figure stood before me. I suddenly felt ................................ . I ................................ stepped inside.

**b)** Insert romantic words to make it sound like a romance novel.

I walked ................................ through the ................................ garden. At both sides of me I saw ................................ plants and ................................ trees. I felt ................................ . In front of me was a ................................ building with a ................................ door. I knocked ................................ . The ................................ door ................................ opened and a ................................ figure stood before me. I suddenly felt ................................ . I ................................ stepped inside.

**c)** Insert jokey and funny words to make it read like a child's fantasy story.

I walked ................................ through the ................................ garden. At both sides of me I saw ................................ plants and ................................ trees. I felt ................................ . In front of me was a ................................ building with a ................................ door. I knocked ................................ . The ................................ door ................................ opened and a ................................ figure stood before me. I suddenly felt ................................ . I ................................ stepped inside.

## Planning a Story

To plan a story you need to identify suitable vocabulary to use. Using each starting word given below, along with a thesaurus, create a word bank of similar vocabulary to help create a consistent mood, tone or style. Then write the opening to a story using the words you've found.

**a)** Describing a mood

   **i)** Words of a similar meaning to **cheerful**:

   **ii)** Story opening:

**b)** Describing appearance

   **i)** Words of a similar meaning to **ugly**:

   **ii)** Story opening:

**c)** Describing a setting

   **i)** Words of a similar meaning to **cold**:

   **ii)** Story opening:

**d)** Describing action

   **i)** Words of a similar meaning to **run**:

   **ii)** Story opening:

## Planning the Parts of a Story

Draw lines between the boxes to match each phrase used in a story with its definition.

**Definition**

a) Part of the story where the plot strands are resolved

b) Disappointment after excitement

c) A problem that often needs to be solved

d) End of the story

e) Where the story is worked out / explained

f) Highlight of the story

g) First part of the story

h) Part of the story leading up to the climax

i) Part of the story that follows the climax

j) Where something unexpected happens

**Phrase**

Introduction

Conclusion

Climax

Twist

Anti-climax

Crisis

Resolution

Denouement

Rising action

Falling action

## Planning the Sequence of a Story

In the table below you have been given an introduction to a story. Complete the table by describing the action that could occur at each part of the story.

| Part of Story | What Happens |
|---|---|
| Introduction | The scene is described – a normal home in the Midlands where a man is writing a book. |
| Rising action | |
| Climax | |
| Falling action | |
| Denouement | |
| Conclusion | |

## Improving your Draft

Here is a draft version of part of a story. It needs to be improved. The author has made some notes to show what needs to be done. Put your answers in the spaces below.

better word needed

what kind of ?

what kind of ?

what kind of ?

add an adjective before 'veil'

adjective needed before 'pile'

add another adjective to go with 'creaking'

check a thesaurus for a more unusual word

add adjective before 'window' meaning 'high up'

better word ?

add adjective before 'book' to make it sound strange

better adverb needed to make me sound more nervous

I walked through the door and saw the room laid out in front of me. The room hadn't been used for years and there was a thin layer of dust over everything, like a veil. In the corner stood a pile of ancient books.

I stepped cautiously over the creaking floorboards towards the centre of the room, which was lit by the strands of light from a window. In the centre of the room stood an old rustic table with an open book placed upon it. The book was open. I ran my finger slowly down the page, scanning to see what it said and to see if it mentioned what I had been looking for. It did.

I _____ through the _____ door and saw the _____ room laid out in front of me. The room hadn't been used for years and there was a thin layer of dust over everything, like a _____ veil. In the corner stood a _____ pile of _____ books.

I stepped cautiously over the _____ creaking floorboards towards the centre of the room, which was lit by the strands of light from a _____ window. In the centre of the room stood a _____ rustic table with an open book placed upon it. The _____ book was open. I ran my finger _____ down the page, scanning to see what it said and to see if it mentioned what I had been looking for. It did.

# Media Texts

## The Language of Text Messages

**1** With a limit on the number of characters that can be used, SMS texts require shorthand and abbreviations. Rewrite the following text messages into good English.

   **a)** Hi. R u cumin 2 c me? Av ad new haircut LOL! Its bad.

   **b)** R u mad? ROTFL IMO ur v.silly

**2** Rewrite the following messages as SMS text messages.

   **a)** This is your mum. I want you to meet me outside the supermarket at 5 o'clock.

   **b)** Do you fancy going to the cinema tonight to see the new Reese Witherspoon film?

## The Language of Email

Are the following statements true or false?

**a)** When you hit 'Reply to All' you send a message to a group of people.

**b)** Business emails are better when they're short because some people have to read a lot in one day.

**c)** It's always OK to be informal in an email.

**d)** Emails always arrive instantly.

**e)** When you put smilies in emails, the person receiving the email will see them the way you do on your computer.

## Newspapers and Magazines

Draw lines between the boxes to match up each newspaper or magazine with its likely audience.

| Audience | Newspaper or Magazine |
|---|---|
| **a)** Older person who enjoys music | Broadsheet newspaper |
| **b)** Male reader with money to spend | Tabloid newspaper |
| **c)** Female reader, perhaps a mother | TV guide |
| **d)** Someone with an interest in one particular band | Chart music magazine |
| **e)** Anyone who owns a property in a particular area | Specialist music magazine |
| **f)** Teenager who enjoys music | Technology magazine |
| **g)** A quite well-educated reader | Home and cooking magazines |
| **h)** A family that tends to stay in | A free local newspaper |
| **i)** People who want easy entertainment from their reading | A fanzine for a band |
| **j)** A reader who wants to find out about the main news issues but who also wants to be entertained | Gossip magazine |

## Research

Research current magazines and newspapers to find the name of one for each of the following audiences.

| Audience | Newspaper or Magazine |
|---|---|
| An older person who enjoys music | |
| A male reader with money to spend | |
| A female reader, perhaps a mother | |
| Someone with an interest in one particular band | |
| Anyone who owns a property in a particular area | |
| A teenager who enjoys music | |

Look at the advert below and match the numbered features with the statements.

② **Innovating for You** ①

③

⑥ *Letts* and **LONSDALE**

⑧ *modern history*

④ Would you like a car combining racing history with modern design? Would you like a car that responds in corners while returning a respectable mpg? The new, improved Lonsdale combines these and more, offering the practicalities of everyday motoring with a tuned yet clean engine.

**Order before September for the special price of £15,995** ← ⑤ **and get free air conditioning and alloy wheels.**

*Car of the Year 2008. European award for Design and Innovation* ← ⑦

A  Use of rhetorical questions to intrigue ☐

B  Company logo stands out ☐

C  Awards listed to support the idea that the car is special ☐

D  Emotive language ☐

E  Object for sale is the biggest thing in the advert ☐

F  Personally addresses the reader ☐

G  Tag-line to make the advert easy to remember ☐

H  Important offer in bold ☐

In video, film and TV there are common abbreviations used for different kinds of camera shots. Match each description to the shot.

1

2

3

4

5

6

7

8

9

10

11

12

**A** EWS – extreme wide shot; often you can't see the subject of the shot.

**B** WS – wide shot; the subject fills the frame from top to bottom.

**C** MS – mid shot; shows some of the subject, but not all of it.

**D** CU – close-up; a certain feature, often the face, fills the shot.

**E** ECU – extreme close-up; close detail.

**F** CA – cutaway; a shot of something other than the current subject.

**G** Cut in; shows some of the subject in detail.

**H** Two-shot; shows two people in as much detail as a mid shot.

**I** OSS – over the shoulder shot; looking from behind a person at the current subject.

**J** POV shot – point of view shot; shows a subject from the subject's point of view.

**K** Weather shot – the weather is shown, perhaps to set the scene.

**L** Noddy shot – a shot in which an interviewer reacts to what the subject is saying.

# Notes